Contents

Front cover: An unusually colorful wild-caught betta. Photo by H.J. Richter.

Front endpaper: A challenging male betta with branchiostegal membrane extended. Photo by Dr. Herbert R. Axelrod.

Frontis: A pair of spawning bettas. Photo by Ruda Zukal.

Back endpaper: A male betta carrying the extended red color trait. Photo by Dr. Herbert R. Axelrod.

Back cover: A young male extended red betta still showing the black edging on the caudal fin. This fish was bred by Mr. and Mrs. L. Bickel. Photo by Al Liebetrau.

ISBN 0-87666-522-9
© 1980 by T.F.H. Publications, Inc.

Distributed in the UNITED STATES by T.F.H. Publications, Inc., 211 West Sylvania Avenue, Neptune City, NJ 07753; in CANADA by H & L Pet Supplies Inc., 27 Kingston Crescent, Kitchener, Ontario N2B 2T6; Rolf C. Hagen Ltd., 3225 Sartelon Street, Montreal 382 Quebec; in ENGLAND by T.F.H. (Great Britain) Ltd., 11 Ormside Way, Holmethorpe Industrial Estate, Redhill, Surrey RH1 2PX; in AUSTRALIA AND THE SOUTH PACIFIC by T.F.H. (Australia) Pty. Ltd., Box 149, Brookvale 2100 N.S.W., Australia; in NEW ZEALAND by Ross Haines & Son, Ltd., 18 Monmouth Street, Grey Lynn, Auckland 2 New Zealand; in SINGAPORE AND MALAYSIA by MPH Distributors Pte., 71-77 Stamford Road, Singapore 0617; in the PHILIPPINES by Bio-Research, 5 Lippay Street, San Lorenzo Village, Makati, Rizal; in SOUTH AFRICA by Multipet Pty. Ltd., 30 Turners Avenue, Durban 4001. Published by T.F.H. Publications Inc., Ltd., the British Crown Colony of Hong Kong. THIS IS THE 1983 EDITION.

BETTAS

BY MARSHALL E. OSTROW

A male betta (lower fish) flares the branchiostegal membranes in a courting gesture toward the female above him. **Below:** A yellow betta tends to its bubblenest overhead.

Introduction

If persistence in the tropical fish hobby is any measure of a fish's popularity, then bettas are by far one of the most popular aquarium fishes ever known. A number of different hobby fishes are just about as beautiful as some of today's highly domesticated bettas, but few have had the long-term popularity of *Betta splendens,* a fish known simply as the betta or by some as the Siamese fighting fish.

Apparently the name Siamese fighting fish, a name well earned by this pugilist, has not thwarted the enthusiasm of hobbyists who keep them. Male bettas instinctively fight with one another, and in the aquarium, where the weaker ones cannot escape as they often can in the wild, only the

strong survive. Although males fight viciously among themselves, one male in a community tank rarely bothers the other species; this may indeed be a contributing factor to the betta's great popularity. As one might expect with such a pugnacious fish, males are quite brutal toward females, even those in spawning condition. Females, like males, tend to fight among themselves but not nearly as intensely as males. It would seem that all of these behavioral problems would cause the betta to parallel the route to oblivion taken by so many other pugnacious fishes that have had only fleeting popularity in the hobby. However, bettas have become, as the result of many years of domestication, one of the most spectacularly beautiful fishes the hobby has ever known and, probably because of that beauty, have remained popular in the hobby almost since its inception.

Records show that modern-day bettas owe a major portion of their good looks to the Orientals who, well over 100 years ago, began to dedicate themselves to developing long finnage and brilliant colors in an otherwise drab wild fish. As with the domestication and culture of goldfish, Oriental families devoted all of their efforts for generations to producing today's long-finned, garish bettas. So highly developed are the bettas of today's aquarium hobby that few novice hobbyists, given the opportunity, would be able to recognize a wild betta as the same species.

Western cultures also contributed their share to the development of this fish that was first described by Regan in 1910. One of the American pioneers in betta development was the late Warren Young, who developed the very long-finned, highly colorful Libby betta which he named in honor of his wife and life-long helpmate, Libby Young. One of the first persons to undertake the scientific study of heredity in the betta was the well-known fish geneticist, the late Dr. Myron Gordon. Other outstanding names such as Dr. Gene Lucas, Drs. Al and Sue Liebetrau, James Sonnier and Walter Maurus have come into recent prominence in

8

connection with new discoveries in the areas of betta genetics and in the development of newer, more beautiful strains of this exotic fish.

In the Orient, and particularly in its native country of Thailand (Siam), the betta's instinctive animosity toward its own kind is capitalized upon through the medium of staged fights in much the same manner as staged cock fights. Considerable sums of money are exchanged in wagers on these fights.

In nature bettas are found in warm steamy swamps and rice paddies. These waters are very poor in oxygen, but bettas have developed the ability to utilize atmospheric oxygen, thus enabling them to live comfortably under conditions in which few other exotic fishes can survive. For this reason domesticated bettas can do with a lot less space than most other hobby fishes, but this does not mean that they can tolerate badly polluted water any better than other fishes. Their ability to survive in cramped quarters is a definite asset for the commercial or semi-commercial breeder when one considers that males over a few months old must be kept isolated from one another.

Siamese fighting fish are one of many species belonging to the large suborder Anabantoidei. Like all fishes belonging to this "air-breathing" group, they are often referred to as anabantoids or often incorrectly as anabantids (the latter are fishes of the family Anabantidae, which bettas are not).

Based upon characteristics common to the members of each family, the suborder Anabantoidei is divided into four families: Anabantidae, Osphronemidae, Helostomatidae and Belontiidae, with bettas belonging to the last named family. The family Belontiidae is subdivided into three separate subfamilies: Belontiinae, Trichogasterinae and Macropodinae. Bettas, paradise fishes, croaking gouramis and several other genera of fishes belong to the subfamily Macropodinae.

Betta imbellis, a naturally occurring species closely related to *Betta splendens*. Photo by E. Roloff. **Below:** The normal red betta has a darkly colored body and a good bit of blue or green iridescence on the body and fins.

Aquarium Conditions

Because of the existence of the labyrinth organ in bettas and other members of these air-breathing families, many aquarists act under the erroneous assumption that these fishes can safely be kept in already overcrowded aquaria. They assume that because the fishes get most of their oxygen from the atmosphere, keeping them in the tank will not further deplete the supply of dissolved oxygen in the water. Not only is this assumption erroneous, but it reflects poor aquarium management, because it can be fatal not only to the betta but also to the other fishes in the tank. Even though bettas don't use as much of the water's dissolved oxygen as other fishes of about the same weight, they do add

about the same amount of water-polluting wastes to the water. Additionally, bettas are just as susceptible to diseases brought on by polluted water as other aquarium fishes are, and in the case of certain diseases such as velvet (which will be covered later) they are perhaps even more susceptible than other fishes.

Many hobbyists prefer to keep bettas in small bowls such as goldfish bowls or large brandy snifters. This is alright if *all* of the bettas' environmental needs are fulfilled, which is not very easy to accomplish in a small bowl. It is therefore best to keep bettas in larger aquaria where they will receive plenty of heat, better water conditions and, in all probability, a better diet.

For reasons reflected upon in the introduction of this book, it is best not to keep more than one male betta in an aquarium, even if it is a very large and heavily planted aquarium. Furthermore, it may even be more hazardous keeping a male and female in the same tank, since the male is just as antagonistic toward a female of his own kind as he is toward a male; the difference is that the female is not as adept at defending herself as a male is.

Most hobbyists find that there is little difficulty keeping any number of female bettas (within the limits of the tank's capacity) in the same aquarium. There may be an occasional shredded fin, but rarely do females inflict severe damage upon one another. Additionally, females are usually far less attractive than males and torn fins are not hereditary, so unless the hobbyist is trying to develop some specimens for a fish show, maintenance of perfect finnage in a female is not as important as it is in a male . . . it is the male that is the showy fish!

WATER TEMPERATURE

When a betta is listless, drab or dark-looking and keeps its fins closed all the time, it is reasonable to assume that the problem is being caused by incorrect water conditions. More often than not the problem is specifically caused by water that is too cool. It was mentioned earlier that in nature bettas are found in swamps and rice paddies in countries such as Thailand where the climate is hot and moist most of the year. Even though domesticated bettas have had many changes bred into them, domestication has not changed their environmental requirements very much. Therefore bettas still need to have very warm water compared to that required by most other ornamental fishes. An aquarium constantly maintained at about 80°F. is a bit too warm for most hobby fishes but not for bettas. In fact, 80°F. is just about ideal for most bettas. Now it becomes obvious why it is so difficult to keep bettas in showy condition in small unheated bowls or brandy snifters. At a room temperature of 70°F. a betta will just lie on the bottom of an aquarium or hide behind the filter. At that temperature it will be very lethargic and will not feed very enthusiastically. In fact, bettas often starve to death at 70°F., no matter what kind of food is being offered. However, gradually raise the temperature to 80°F. and a remarkable transformation takes place. That drab dark blob from the bottom of the tank suddenly comes to life—it begins to swim actively with its fins open . . . its colors lighten and brighten to a spectacular brilliance (especially in a male) . . . it becomes alert, responding quickly to all stimuli around it . . . it feeds almost gluttonously. The difference between a cool betta and a warm betta is so marked that once you've seen the difference you'll never again keep a betta in unheated water. A tank heated to 82 or 83°F. is not too warm to stimulate breeding in these fish.

Very mild aeration from a selectively located airstone is important in the betta tank, not necessarily to supplement the oxygen supply as would be the case with most fishes kept in water this warm, but to prevent the heated water from stratifying. In other words, the heat in the aquarium should be uniform throughout the tank, and this will not be the case unless the water is circulated.

(1) This betta, bred by Jim Sonnier, carries the melano trait which accounts for its lacy blackish fins, and it also carries the butterfly trait. (2) A multicolor betta carrying an excessively heavy amount of iridescent green pigment. (3) A Cambodian red-white butterfly betta. While it is a good specimen, it would be perfect if the red patches on the fins were separated away from the body. (4) A sturdy young extended red female ripe for spawning (bred by Mr. and Mrs. L. Bickel.) Photos by Al Liebetrau.

WATER CHEMISTRY

Water hardness and pH, although not as critical as temperature where breeding and raising bettas are concerned, are quite important. In nature bettas are found in fairly soft waters that are neutral to slightly acidic; rarely is the water alkaline. In captivity bettas seem to be quite flexible in their water hardness and pH requirements as long as extremes are avoided. Water having a hardness of 2 DH to about 12 DH (degrees of hardness) and a pH value of 6.4 to about 7.4 seems to be tolerated quite well. I have successfully bred bettas many times in ordinary tap water having a pH of 7.0 to 7.2 and a DH of 8 to 12. However, I know some hobbyists who swear by soft acid water, water having a pH of 6.4 and a DH of 2 to 4. I don't believe there really is a right or wrong water composition for raising bettas, as long as extremes are avoided.

For those interested in using soft acidic water for their bettas, the best way to achieve this condition is to run the water through peat moss that has been sandwiched between two layers of filter floss in either an outside power filter or in an inside box filter until the desired chemistry is attained. Make sure the peat moss used is safe for aquarium use. Some brands of peat moss, especially those purchased in a garden shop, are treated with fungus-retarding chemicals or other preservatives. This kind of peat moss can be lethal to your bettas. If the bag the peat moss is packaged in makes no mention of added chemicals, it is generally safe to use. Just to be sure, however, stay with the peat moss products that are sold in tropical fish shops for the purposes mentioned here.

Although bettas have a wide tolerance for various levels of pH and water hardness, they are no more tolerant of pollutants such as ammonia, hydrogen sulfide, carbon dioxide and nitrites than any other fishes. That they are more tolerant of these pollutants is a delusion that many hobbyist operate under, probably because they know that bettas can breathe atmospheric oxygen. However, what these misinformed hobbyists fail to realize is that these pollutants cause other problems besides asphyxiation. Excesses of ammonia and nitrites, for instance, can destroy delicate gill membranes and can even affect the labyrinth organ. Excesses of pollutants in the water can put bettas, or any other fishes for that matter, under severe environmental stress, thus making them much more susceptible to diseases such as ich, velvet, bacterial fin rot and bacterial gill diseases than they would be if they were kept in pollutant-free water.

FILTRATION AND AERATION

Special consideration must be given to bettas where water circulation is concerned. It was mentioned earlier that in nature bettas are found in swamps and rice paddies, and they are also found in drainage ditches and small stagnant pools. They are obviously quite well adapted to these habitats and accordingly cannot handle swift currents or fast-moving water. For this reason aeration and filtration should be quite mild. The problem of water movement is especially difficult for domesticated bettas that have very long, flowing fins. I have seen bettas behave rather lethargically when kept under all of the right conditions except for water movement. Yet as soon as the water circulation was reduced to just a bit more than a trickle, the very same bettas became transformed into active colorful fish in much the same way they would by raising their water temperature from 70 to 80°F.

As long as there are plenty of plants and other decorations in the community tank, bettas can be kept there without much difficulty, because the objects in the tank break up some of the currents created by filters. However, if a betta is being kept in a relatively barren tank such as a special breeding or rearing tank, the strength of the filtration should be reduced. In other words, don't use a power filter in such a tank.

1

(1) The vertical bars on this ripe blue female betta indicate her readiness to spawn. Photo by Al Liebetrau. (2) This dark blue male is attractive, but, because of the excess red in its fins, it is not a show quality betta.

2

3

(3) A dark blue male showing the combtail trait. (4) A double-tail dark blue male bred by Dr. Larry Baum. Photos by Al Liebetrau.

4

Undergravel filters and box filters can be used successfully in betta rearing tanks if they are installed properly. Make sure the riser tubes of these filters reach from the filters themselves up to the surface of the water. This maximizes the efficiency of these filters. Some of these filters are available with a 90° elbow that is installed at the top of the riser tube. These help increase water circulation by directing filtered water across the surface and at the same time control excessive turbulence that could be disturbing to bettas. Such an arrangement also helps dissipate into the atmosphere polluting gases such as carbon dioxide. With undergravel filters it is also important to be sure the gravel is deep enough. Since these are essentially biological filters, there must be enough substrate material to which the bacterial colonies that degrade the wastes can adhere. A gravel depth of between two and three inches is correct. Less than that does not provide enough substrate for the bacteria. More than that slows down the water circulation through the gravel, making the filter less effective.

Undergravel filters should not be used in a betta breeding tank because the use of gravel on the bottom of the tank makes it difficult for the male to find the very tiny eggs that sink to the bottom during spawning. Filtration in the breeding tank is covered in greater detail in the breeding section of this book.

If filtration in the betta tank is set up properly, it is not necessary to further aerate the tank using an airstone. However, some breeders prefer to use mild aeration from an airstone in lieu of any filtration in the breeding tank. This, too, is covered in detail in the breeding section of this book.

(1) A typical Thailand swampland habitat of *Betta splendens*. (2) A commercial betta-breeding establishment in Thailand. Water is changed in these jars almost daily by the owner's helpers.

Rotifers hidden in a mat of filamentous algae. Rotifers are one of many kinds of tiny organisms that can be used as food for betta fry. Photo by Charles O. Masters. **Below:** A trophy-winning turquoise (green) betta bred by Mr. and Mrs. Gary Dowdy. An assortment of live and nutritious prepared foods is necessary to raise a fine show specimen such as this. Photo by Al Liebetrau.

Foods and Feeding

Once the aquarist gets past the problems caused by the "new tank syndrome," a new set of problems often arises—problems caused by improper nutrition. No matter how well an aquarium is maintained and no matter how correct the water conditions are for the species being kept, a fish will not remain in good health for very long if its dietary needs are not met.

The key to healthy bettas is proper diet. Bettas that are fed well (considering quality as well as quantity) are much more resistant to diseases than bettas that are raised on an unbalanced diet. In addition, well-fed bettas have much more tolerance for the occasional pollutants they may be exposed to than do malnourished bettas.

The answer to the question of how to provide bettas with a well-rounded diet lies first in understanding something about the foods they feed upon in nature and second in providing them with a similar assortment of nutrients in the aquarium.

Combining knowledge of the betta's natural environment with some knowledge of the betta's basic anatomy will help one understand what and how bettas eat. One of the most prominent anatomical features of the betta is its upturned mouth. One may surmise from this that bettas cannot feed at the bottom of an aquarium, but they can feed at the bottom as well as at the surface. However, in a competitive situation, for instance in a community aquarium where there may be well-adapted bottom-feeding fishes as well as good surface feeders, bettas will not compete very well with bottom-feeding fishes for food particles that reach the bottom. On the other hand, they will out-compete most predominantly bottom-feeding fishes for foods that remain at the surface.

A less obvious anatomical feature of the betta is its relatively short alimentary tract. Such a digestive system is usually associated with a carnivorous fish. Fishes that tend to be herbivorous, such as mollies, usually have a proportionately longer alimentary tract.

Now consider the betta's habitats, which were already described as warm stagnant pools, swamps, drainage ditches and rice paddies. In such an environment mosquitos and other insects that rely upon stagnant bodies of water for reproduction are quite predominant. In the water, and especially near the surface, their larvae are abundant. These larvae as well as small insects that light upon or fall into the water comprise the mainstay of the betta's diet in nature. Their great availability and the betta's natural ability to devour them makes such insects and their larvae the ideal food for bettas.

In the aquarium, of course, it is not possible to provide

bettas with either the variety or the quantity of insects they consume in the wild, so other foods must be substituted. However, in selecting substitutes it is not possible to find one food that provides the betta with all of the nutritional components found in the great variety of creatures that bettas devour in the wild. Therefore it is necessary to feed captive and domesticated bettas a great variety of substitute foods to ensure that they receive at least some of the different kinds of proteins as well as the fats, carbohydrates, fiber, vitamins and minerals that they need for proper growth, reproduction and the maintenance of good health.

A diet consisting of only one kind of food or even only a few kinds of foods is bound to cause malnutrition in fishes. Although the effects of malnutrition may not always be obvious to the hobbyist, they may be seen in lowered disease resistance, poor color, poor growth and poor reproductive ability.

Although a high-protein diet in fishes is quite important, other dietary components are important too. For instance, a fish kept on a high-protein diet which does not have sufficient carbohydrates will show very poor growth. This is because carbohydrates have a protein-sparing effect. In other words, a fish that is not getting sufficient carbohydrates must utilize the proteins it is consuming to maintain metabolism instead of using proteins for growth.

Although the fat requirements of warm water fishes are rather low, they must have some fat in the diet. Fats provide concentrated energy and are also protein-sparing. In addition they assist a fish in maintaining neutral buoyancy.

Minerals play important roles in bone formation, fluid regulation, ionic balance and operation of the nervous system. A variety of minerals is required in the diet of fishes.

Fiber, usually vegetable fiber has an essential role even in the diet of carnivorous fishes such as bettas. It extends or dilutes the concentration of other dietary components so as to prevent gastric disorders caused by an overly rich diet.

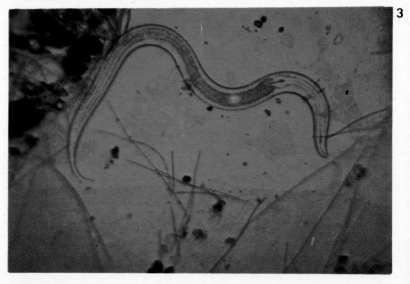

(1) *Paramecium* are microscopic organisms that make ideal food for betta fry. (2) Finely sifted young *Daphnia* can be eaten by young bettas that have already been feeding for a week or two. (3) Microworms are small enough to be used as a first food for betta fry. (4) Hydra are freshwater relatives of anemones and should be kept out of aquaria in which fishes are being bred, for a hydra is capable of capturing and devouring betta fry. Hydra can be introduced into the aquarium on aquatic plants or with food. (5) Although bettas are well built for surface feeding, they have very little difficulty eating tubifex worms that have fallen to the bottom of the aquarium. Photos 1, 3 and 5 by Charles O. Maters. Photo 4 by Dr. H. Reichenbach-Klinke.

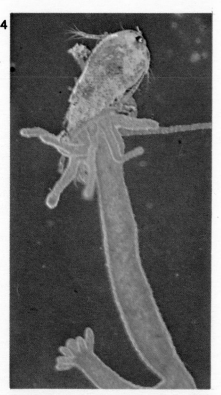

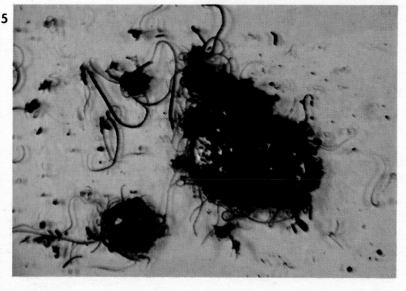

Chitin, which is a principle component of the exoskeleton of the insects eaten by bettas, provides much of this dietary dilution but not all of it. Many of the creatures eaten by bettas have undigested vegetable matter in their digestive tracts. Thus indirectly bettas consume vegetable matter, hence fiber.

Vitamins, of course, have very basic roles in the diets of all animals, for they aid in maintaining the normal processes that occur in most tissue. Without the proper assortment of vitamins, overt deficiency diseases can result. For example, fishes that lack riboflavin in the diet are prone to eye problems such as a cloudy lens or hemorrhagic spots, poor growth, skin and fin hemorrhages, dark coloration and anemia. Fishes lacking vitamin A are prone to exophthalmos (pop-eye), kidney hemorrhages and poor growth.

A variety of foods in the diet of bettas ensures that all of the dietary components just mentioned are included. Many of these components can be provided in commercially prepared dry flake or pellet foods. There is quite a variety of them available, some containing specialized ingredients for the promotion of growth, some for color, some for conditioning, some with a concentration of one type of ingredient such as plankton, greens, shrimp or tubifex worms and some containing a general nutritious mixture of many ingredients. It is advisable to keep at least three or four different kinds of dry foods on hand all the time and they should be used regularly, in rotation, as a part of the daily feeding schedule.

Another useful form of dry food is freeze-dried food. Like the flake and pellet foods, freeze-dried foods are easy to use and can be stored for a long time if they are kept in airtight, moisture-proof containers, which is what most of them are packaged in. Freeze-dried foods are also high in nutrition and are available in a number of different forms. Freeze-dried brine shrimp, tubifex worms, plankton, *Daphnia* and several other organisms are commercially available in tropical fish shops. They, too, can be included as a regular part of the diet.

Frozen foods such as clams, mussels, shrimp, squid, mosquito larvae, bloodworms (chironomid or midge larvae), glassworms (*Chaoborus* or phantom midge larvae), newly hatched and adult brine shrimp, ocean plankton, kelp and beef heart are available in convenient packages at most tropical fish shops. Even marine foods are useful in raising bettas as long as they are not used as the mainstay of the diet.

Many of these items as well as other varieties of foods can be prepared and frozen at home. Fish, shellfish and raw meats of almost any kind (as long as they are nearly but not entirely fat-free) can be used. The food can be frozen in small blocks and scraped into the aquarium using a single-edged razor blade or a sharp knife, or it can be chopped in a blender or food processor and frozen in thin sheets after the liquid is rinsed out through a strainer or a piece of cheese-cloth. For the latter process it helps if you use a butterknife or the handle of a spoon to score the sheet of food when it is partially frozen. The score marks should divide the sheet so that when it is completely frozen it can easily be broken into meal-size blocks for convenient storage in a plastic container.

Whether purchased already prepared or prepared at home, as many different kinds of frozen foods as possible should be included on a regular basis in the betta's diet.

LIVE FOODS

Some hobbyists have had a lot of success breeding and rearing bettas without ever using any kind of live food. More often than not, however, the bigger, more colorful, fancy-finned specimens result from a diet abundant in live foods. When the importance of live food is emphasized for a successful breeding program, many hobbyists shy away, envisioning themselves in soaking wet tennis shoes and

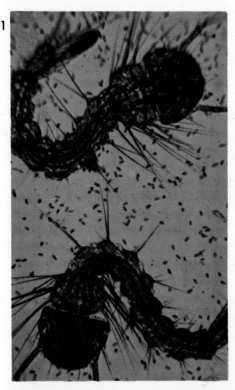

A variety of live food helps produce healty, robust bettas. (1) During the spring, summer and fall mosquito larvae are readily available and are a favorite food of bettas. (2) Live adult brine shrimp are available in pet shops all over the country. (3) Small black ants make excellent food for surface-feeding fishes such as bettas. (4) Bloodworms are actually the larvae of midges which are a type of terrestrial fly. They can be found in the bottom muck of ponds, and when well washed they make an excellent, highly nutritious food for bettas. (5) White-worms are a good conditioning food for potential breeder bettas. They are easily cultivated in a box of garden soil. Photo 1, 2, 4 and 5 by Charles O. Masters.

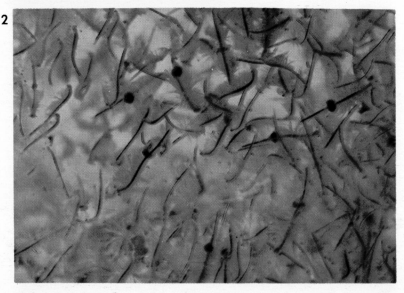

knee-deep in mud with snapping turtles and predatory fishes chomping away at their ankles and knees as they try to net a few *Daphnia* for their fishes. This may have been what the hobby was like 50 years ago, but it certainly isn't today, especially if you live in or near a large metropolitan area.

A visit to many tropical fish shops reveals live adult brine shrimp and tubifex worms shipped in fresh twice a week and readily available to hobbyists for a mere $.35 to $.50 per portion. With the cost of transportation to get to suitable collecting sites being what it is, it hardly seems worth getting live food for your bettas anywhere but at your local tropical fish shop. Not only do dealers sell live foods that are immediately consumable, but some also sell organisms such as whiteworms, microworms and "wingless" or vestigal-winged fruitflies all of which can be easily cultivated so as to provide a continuous supply of live food.

For hobbyists who have no aversion to hiking in the woods and wading in shallow ponds and swamps, collecting your own live foods is not nearly as unpleasant as it may seem on first thought. As a matter of fact, it can be a lot of fun and can help put you into close touch with the needs and requirements of your fishes. During the spring, summer and fall mosquito larvae, bloodworms, *Daphnia* and several other organisms can be collected, even close to or within large cities! During the winter and at some of the same collecting sites visited during the summer, glassworms and a few other organisms can be collected. As long as the collecting areas are not badly polluted, it is not necessary to drive miles into the country to collect live foods for your bettas.

The only special knowledge that is required to collect your own live foods is what kinds of habitats to find them in and how to avoid introducing into your aquaria potential fish enemies that might be lurking among the organisms in your food collection. This information is readily available

THE WORLD'S LARGEST SELECTION OF PET, ANIMAL, AND MUSIC BOOKS.

T.F.H. Publications publishes more than 900 books covering many hobby aspects (dogs, cats, birds, fish, small animals, music, etc.). Whether you are a beginner or an advanced hobbyist you will find exactly what you're looking for among our complete listing of books. For a free catalog fill out the form on the other side of this page and mail it today.

. . CATS . . .

. . . BIRDS . .

. . . ANIMALS . . .

. . . DOGS . . .

. . FISH . . .

. . . MUSIC . . .

For more than 30 years, *Tropical Fish Hobbyist* has been the source of accurate, up-to-the-minute, and fascinating information on every facet of the aquarium hobby.

Join the more than 50,000 devoted readers worldwide who wouldn't miss a single issue.

(1) There are commercially prepared dry foods that are excellent as part of the diet of growing young bettas. (2) For young adult and adult bettas an assortment of commercially manufactured freeze-dried foods are available. Several of them should be included in every bettas's diet.

in any number of articles that have appeared over the years in *The Tropical Fish Hobbyist* magazine. In addition, the collection and culturing of live foods are discussed in simple but very detailed presentations in *Encyclopedia of Live Foods* by Charles O. Masters.

Whether you choose to hatch your own brine shrimp or buy it live, cultivate other live foods or collect them from their natural habitats, it is advisable not to neglect this important aspect of fish keeping and breeding. The use of live foods at least several times a week in the diet of your bettas will produce results second to none in terms of good growth, vivid coloration and a high reproductive rate as well as general good health and resistance to disease.

33

Hyphae of the fungus *Saprolegnia.* This and several other similar kinds of fungi readily attack open wounds on bettas. Photo by D. McDaniel. **Below:** Young swarmers of *Ichthyophthirius multifiliis.* This is the infective stage in the life cycle of the ich parasite. Photo by Dr. H. Reichenbach-Klinke.

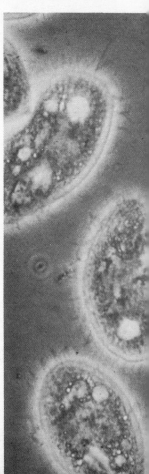

Diseases: Prevention, Diagnosis, Treatment

Although the tropical fish hobby has been in existence as a hobby for well over 50 years, the diagnosis and treatment of diseases in fishes are only in their infancy. Much is known about some of the common fish diseases such as ich or velvet and how to treat fishes having these diseases, but there are many more diseases to which ornamental fishes are subject and about which little is known at all. However, more often than not good aquarium management can prevent the occurrence of rare diseases in the aquarium, as it can similarly prevent the occurrence of some of the more common diseases.

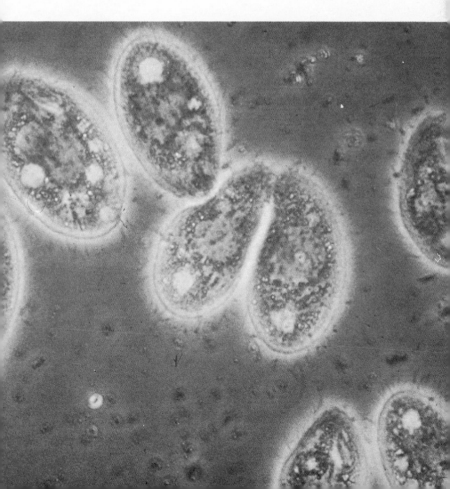

Prevention, not treatment, is the key to good aquarium management. Prevention is usually far easier to effect than cure and can be accomplished by simply keeping the fishes out of stressful environmental situations. Any time a fish is placed under stress by either chemical or physical means it is weakened and experiences shock to varying degrees of intensity, depending upon the severity of the cause. In a shocked condition a fish is much more susceptible to attack by disease organisms than it is in good health. Many disease organisms survive well in a healthy aquarium but do not proliferate until conditions become suitable for their reproduction. A shocked or stressed fish is one of the suitable conditions for their proliferation. It takes only one weakened fish to produce a bloom of disease organisms of sufficient magnitude to cause even healthy, unstressed fishes to succumb to the disease. Once some of the formerly healthy fishes succumb, the disease begins to snowball and can reach such magnitude that none of the standard treatments or remedies are the least bit effective in destroying the disease.

A further complication in treating fish diseases is the variance in a given fish's reaction to the medication due to intrinsic species characteristics; for example, some small tetras cannot tolerate a standard malachite green treatment for ich. Other fishes' reactions to medication may vary due to improper environmental conditions or poor diet. The point is that very often a treated fish can die from the cure, thus it is well worth the effort required to prevent the disease in the first place.

Preventive maintenance is not difficult to practice, even when many small containers are being used to house individual male bettas. It is most important in preventing diseases that fish not be subjected to the stress caused by polluted water. Water pollution can be reduced by careful feeding and not allowing any uneaten food to remain in the aquarium for more than a few minutes. A dead fish or any kind of decomposing organic matter should be removed from the aquarium as soon as it is spotted. Allowing a dead fish to remain in the tank for the other fishes or scavenger snails to pick apart is a serious mistake. Any organic matter that is not living should be removed from the aquarium as soon as it is noticed. This kind of preventive maintenance reduces the load on aquarium filters and helps produce very stable chemical conditions in the water.

Unfluctuating warm temperatures are another major factor in keeping bettas disease-free. Sudden temperature changes or prolonged exposure to water that is too cool will produce shock in a betta, thus making it very susceptible to velvet (one of the most common diseases of bettas) and other diseases. In tropical Southeast Asia, the natural home of the betta, the water temperature rarely fluctuates more than a few degrees from day to day or even season to season. For this reason even domesticated bettas are not tolerant of wide temperature fluctuations.

In the chapter on foods and feeding the importance of a high quality varied diet was emphasized as a way of preventing disease outbreaks in ornamental fishes. I shall emphasize this again only by saying that there are very few diseases, bacterial, viral, protozoan or otherwise, that a malnourished fish can resist successfully.

The best way to prevent water pollution caused by a buildup of fish wastes and uneaten food particles, in addition of course to a good filtering system, is by making regular partial water changes. If a proper feeding schedule is rigidly followed, a weekly change of one-fourth to one-third of the aquarium water will keep wastes sufficiently diluted. The replacement water can be drawn at the correct temperature from the tap and placed directly in the aquarium without dechlorination if no more than one-third of the original water is replaced at one time. This is because the remaining old water sufficiently dilutes the chlorine. If more than one-third of the water must be replaced, it should first be dechlorinated either by aging or by the use of a chemical sold by pet shops for that purpose.

No matter how well an aquarium is maintained, there are bound to be times that certain diseases will infect your bettas. In order to stop the progress of these diseases before they become fatal, you must be able to recognize their early symptoms so that you can begin the proper treatment immediately. This is not always easy to do, for many diseases produce no direct signs of their presence until they have had a few days to develop in or on the host fish. However, with most aquarium fishes there are early signs of stress that are common to many diseases; if these signs are recognized early enough, the disease outbreak can be prevented entirely.

Learn to recognize the normal appearance of your bettas. You should know, for instance, how fast and how far the gill covers and mouth move during normal respiration in order to recognize when the fish is breathing too fast or too laboriously. Labored or rapid breathing is one of the first signs of ammonia poisoning or other chemical imbalances in the water. It is also one of the first signs of bacterial gill diseases or ich. If the fish is flashing or glancing off objects in the aquarium, this is an attempt to relieve a skin irritation caused either by a parasite or by chemical irritants in the water. If the fish's fins appear more ragged than normal or even split, it could be suffering from a dietary deficiency or a bacterial or fungal infection. There are many other early signs of trouble, but since this is not a book on fish diseases, I shall not attempt to list them all here. There are many good fish health books available to help you recognize fish diseases. Although these books can be helpful, they should not be used as a substitute for daily observation of your bettas. If one gets to know the normal behavior and appearance of his fishes intimately, it becomes quite easy to recognize when something has gone awry.

When it is detected that the fish is behaving abnormally

in some way or shows sores, wounds, darkened areas or any other skin abnormalities, the fish should immediately be isolated from the others if it is not already being kept in its own aquarium. This will very often prevent the spread of a contagious disease to other fishes and will make it easier for you to observe the afflicted fish. Once the disease progresses far enough for a diagnosis to be made, immediate treatment can be administered.

Medications should be used with great caution and discretion, for their overuse can affect fishes in much the same way that overuse of a drug affects humans. For instance, if an antibiotic is being used to treat a bacterial infection and it is used too often, it may be useless at a time when it is critically needed, because the bacteria in question may have developed an immunity to the drug. Eliminating that which caused the bacteria to proliferate in the first place, for instance an accumulation of uneaten food or an overcrowded aquarium, along with the first treatment of the infected fish makes more sense than ignoring the cause and continuing to medicate the fish for a prolonged period of time.

It is not a good idea to try to hurry a cure in an ailing fish by bombarding it with an array of medications or by increasing the dosage over that recommended by the manufacturer of the drug. In most cases the recommended dosage is enough to kill the disease organisms without harming the fish. An increased dosage might kill the disease organisms faster in some cases but is also likely to produce harmful side effects in the fish or perhaps even kill it. There are some cases in which two or more medications used simultaneously have beneficial effects on the fish being treated. In other words, the medications act together in a way that neither one of them would act if given separately. However, this cooperative action can have harmful effects on the fish too. Most manufacturers have a lot of research behind their drug combinations, but the hobbyist should not take it upon himself to make such combinations.

Even if one is lucky enough not to harm the fish by increasing the dosage or by adding additional medications to the treatment, it is not always possible to shorten the cure time. Certain disease organisms have only a limited period in their life cycle during which they are susceptible to the effects of killing medications. Therefore, these organisms must be allowed to run their course if their life cycle is to be broken.

In some instances diseases or wounds are of such proportions that any attempt to medicate is useless. Though it is no doubt emotionally painful for the fish's owner to destroy it, this is sometimes the best course of action. Prolonging the fish's life in this case could increase the chances of the disease spreading to fishes in other tanks and could cost the hobbyist a lot of time and money for naught, in addition to tying up needed tank space.

Hopelessly ailing fishes can be destroyed quickly and almost painlessly by using any of several commonly employed methods. Some hobbyists prefer to place the fish in a net and dip it into boiling water. Others prefer to wrap the fish in a plastic bag or in plastic wrap and either give it a sharp blow with a hard object or quickly throw it against a hard surface. By either method the ailing fish dies almost instantly and therefore feels very little, if any, pain. It should be noted that a fish's nervous system is not nearly as highly developed as that of a higher animal, so the likelihood of a fish "feeling" pain as we know pain is rather remote.

Disposing of a diseased fish should be done with the greatest of care. The carcass should be incinerated or wrapped in a leak-proof plastic bag and either thrown in the garbage or buried. This will help prevent the possibility of any fish disease spreading to fishes inhabiting natural water systems. Diseased fishes should not be flushed down the toilet!

If a contagious fish disease is detected in the aquarium, the diseased fishes, as mentioned earlier, should be isolated from the healthy ones. Sometimes, however, isolation is not enough to prevent the further spread of the disease among the other fishes. In that case all of the fishes may have to be removed from the tank, with the infected ones isolated from the non-infected ones, and the aquarium broken down and sterilized. All of the non-organic items in the tank such as the gravel, heater, filter, thermometer, plastic plants and rocks can be left in the tank for sterilization. This can be done by draining the aquarium (with the heater unplugged, naturally) and refilling it with a very strong saline solution. As much salt as can be dissolved in the water will kill most freshwater pathogens. It is probably best to use non-iodized salt for a freshwater aquarium. Sterilizing solutions such as formalin (the liquid form of formaldehyde), methylene blue or potassium permanganate can be used. If formalin is used, the aquarium must be tightly covered as one can easily be overcome by the acrid odor. If methylene blue or potassium permanganate is used one must be aware that these chemicals can leave permanent stains on plastics and even on the gravel. Whichever sterilizing solution is chosen, a 24-hour soak is best. *Never* use hot water to sterilize or clean an aquarium, as it will cause the glass to crack! Live plants can be sterilized by soaking them no longer than five minutes in a solution of alum, a product available from most pharmacies. Mix a tablespoon of alum to a quart of room-temperature water. The plants should be rinsed thoroughly after the five-minute soak.

There are many diseases, contagious and non-contagious as well as curable and non-curable, that can affect bettas. Because of obvious space limitations they cannot all be discussed in this book, so only a few of the more common diseases of bettas will be discussed.

WHITE SPOT

There are probably very few aquarists who have not at

one time or another been faced with an outbreak of white spot disease or "ich" in their tanks. The persistence of this disease has probably caused more people to drop out of the tropical fish hobby than any other single problem. It is caused by a ciliated protozoan parasite called *Ichthyophthirius multifiliis*. The disease is seen as small white spots about the size of grains of salt or sugar on the body and fins of its victim. Each white spot is an encysted parasite that is or has been feeding upon the body fluids of its host fish.

Once the feeding period is over the cyst drops off the fish and falls to the bottom. At this stage reproduction has already begun within the cyst; usually about 24 hours after the cyst falls off the fish, it breaks open and releases hundreds of new free-swimming parasites. Each new parasite seeks out a host upon which to feed. Any fish that has just undergone any kind of shock is a likely candidate. This is why an ich outbreak so very often follows a sudden chilling in an aquarium. A sudden drop of even a few degrees of temperature can cause a fish's resistance to ich to break down completely.

The only part of the life cycle of this parasite during which it is vulnerable to treatment is the brief free-swimming stage. For this reason any treatment must be continued for about ten days even though all of the white spots may be long gone from the fish. The parasite cannot be killed during its feeding and reproduction cycles by any means that would not also kill the host fish.

One of the best ways to break the life cycle of ich parasites is by elevating the aquarium temperature to about 86°F. At that temperature the free-swimmers usually cannot survive long enough to attach to a host. The host fish's resistance can be increased somewhat by adding about a teaspoon of salt to each gallon of its water. At 86° F the water must be aerated fairly well, for at that temperature it holds very little dissolved oxygen and in such water even bettas may have a difficult time breathing. It also helps break the life cycle of the parasites during this treatment if all of the fishes are removed and treated in a separate aquarium. The heat application should be continued in the original aquarium. This whole procedure assures that no free-swimmers will find a host, so, even if they survive the heat, they will die of starvation.

Ich can be treated chemically in bettas by the judicious use of a chemical called malachite green. It is available alone or in a proven beneficial combination with other chemicals and is sold in tropical fish shops under a variety of trade names. If the primary ingredient of the medication is malachite green, then it is to be used for the treatment of fishes having ich. The treatment must be continued for about ten days for the same reason that any other treatment must be continued that long.

VELVET DISEASE

Bettas are highly susceptible to velvet *(Oodinium)*, which is first seen as a golden to yellowish granular area along the back. It spreads rapidly, eventually covering most of the fish's body and fins, and is a highly contagious disease that can be easily transmitted to other aquaria by not thoroughly washing and disinfecting the hands or equipment such as nets that might be interchanged between tanks.

Like ich, velvet is a protozoan parasite that has a definite life cycle. It can be treated, but, as in treating ich, the treatment must be continued for at least ten days to break the cycle. Infected fish respond to treatment with copper sulfate. This can be purchased as a prepared fish medication, and a recommended dosage is given by each manufacturer. Another effective medication is acriflavine. This pharmaceutical dye is also sold as a fish medication and comes with specific dosage instructions.

BACTERIAL FIN ROT

As the name implies, this is a bacterial infection of the

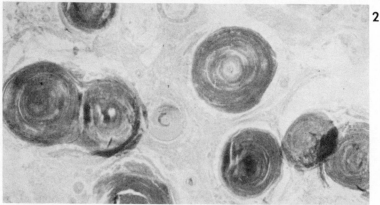

(1) Breeding usually results in considerable fin and body damage to female bettas. After breeding, females should be kept in an aquarium that is as sterile as possible until the wounds begin to heal. Photo by G. Senfft. (2) This is a tissue sample taken from a betta infected with the spores of an *Ichthyosporidium* parasite (dark circles). Ths disease caused by this parasite is called ichthyophonus and is generally not curable. Photo by Dr. R. Geisler.

fins. It usually attacks the outer edges of the fins first, especially the caudal fin. The bacteria causing the disease usually proliferate in aquaria that are not kept very clean, for instance in an aquarium in which a lot of fish feces and uneaten food have been allowed to accumulate.

The best treatment for this disease is a wide-spectrum antibiotic such as Tetracycline® dissolved in the water. This and several other antibiotics are available in tropical fish shops. As mentioned before, antibiotics should not be used very often or the bacteria will build up an immunity to their killing action. It is much better to treat the disease once and clean up the source of the bacteria.

FUNGUS
Although there are some fungal diseases that are primary infections, the fungus we are concerned with here is an external secondary infection. It is seen as a white edging along ragged fins that have been attacked by a bacterial infection. This fungus, often of the genus *Saprolegnia* or closely related types, attacks tissue that is already dead, but it can destroy live tissue too. The infection can also be seen as cottony tufts along the body, on the eyes and around or in the mouth of its victims. Fungi often attack the site of a wound on a fish.

One of the best ways to rid a fish of a *Saprolegnia* infection is to place the fish in a fairly strong saline solution (four tablespoons of salt per gallon of water) until it begins to show stress. It should then be removed, held in a net or soft soap-free cloth that is soaked in fresh water and the infection sites swabbed with a disinfectant such as Mercurochrome® or Argyrol® . The disinfectant should not be permitted to flow into the fish's gill chambers. After allowing the disinfectant to work for 15 to 30 seconds, the fish should be returned to a clean well-filtered aquarium. The treatment can be repeated every few hours and should be continued until there are no further signs of fungus growing on the fish.

The diseases mentioned in this section are the ones that occur most commonly in bettas. There are many other diseases that can attack them; some are curable and some are not. It is advisable for all aquarists to have at least one book on fish diseases handy. A good book for thorough yet simplified information on disease diagnosis and treatment is Dr. G. Schubert's book *Cure and Recognize Aquarium Fish Diseases.*

A betta that does not show this active state of arousal when confronted by another betta in an adjacent jar should not be purchased, for it may be past its breeding prime. Photo by K. Paysan. **Below:** Commercial betta breeders as well as retailers usually keep bettas in small jars. Hobbyists should not keep bettas in small containers unless the room they are kept in is well heated.

Purchasing Bettas

Although genetics or inheritance no doubt plays a major role in determining what a mature betta looks like, certain environmental factors should not be overlooked in their importance toward this determination. Factors such as food, living space, water chemistry, temperature and even the age of the breeding parents all contribute toward the final appearance of a mature betta.

For this reason bettas stocked in pet shops should not be overlooked as a potential source of good breeding stock, provided that only young bettas are purchased. While the retailer, because of his rapid turnover of stock, cannot always provide ideal conditions for his bettas, you, the hobbyist, can. Therefore, if a betta seen in a shop shows pro-

mise but lacks some of the qualities you desire, it may still be a good buy, because you may be able to add those missing qualities by simply improving the fish's environment. This, of course, is only possible if you are dealing with a young specimen. An old betta may have distorted or kinked fins and poor color, and these faults cannot be improved upon very much no matter what environmental modifications are made. In addition, an older betta may be past its reproductive prime. It is, therefore, very helpful to know in terms of age, size, shape and color what to look for when selecting bettas from a shop or from the fish room of a friend.

PROPORTIONS

If you are dealing with a friend or a known breeder, it is easy to find out how old the bettas are; simply ask! If the person is someone you trust, the matter need not be questioned any further. However, it still pays to know the signs of a young or old fish. This is especially true when purchasing bettas from a dealer, because the dealer buys his fish from a wholesaler or from various commercial breeders and cannot always know exactly how old the stock is.

A young betta generally has smooth body lines with no unusual curves along the back and no rough-looking scales. Older bettas generally have what I can only describe as an *older look* which includes a thicker, no-so-smooth-looking body and some rough-looking scales. Younger specimens generally have smoother lines to the fins, too, and the caudal, anal and dorsal fins are usually a bit rounder in shape than they are in older specimens. For the novice, an old betta and a youngster must be viewed side by side in order to distinguish the difference. After a bit of practice, however, it is easy to spot the "senior citizens of bettadom."

An older betta may have been bred a few times or may have had a few contacts with other males and often shows battle scars such as kinks in the fin rays where the fin may

48

have been torn and healed (they rarely heal up as smoothly as they were in the first place). This does not mean that you should eliminate from consideration all bettas having kinked fins. A young fish can sustain injuries, too, and while such a fish may not become a good show specimen, it could be an excellent breeder if it has all of the other desired traits. The kinked fins could, however, be a hereditary condition. You will learn to distinguish the difference as you progress in your specialized pursuit.

While fin length is certainly an important consideration in choosing a male betta, fullness of the fins is equally important. Long fins that taper in such a way that the outer edge is much narrower than the fin base could be a hereditary condition or could be the result of a poor diet. Whatever the reason for fish having fins of this type, it should be rejected as a potential breeder. The caudal fin should have a roundish shape. The anal fin should almost have the shape of a parallelogram so that it seemingly merges with the caudal fin. A draped shape to the fins, even when they are spread, often indicates good stock. Fin rays that extend beyond the edge of the fin tissue between the rays suggests that you are looking at a sturdy fish. This characteristic should be fairly uniform all along the outer edge of the fin; bettas whose fins have an irregular or ragged edge will not take very many show trophies. Curled tips and curled edges on the fins are also undesirable traits. Sometimes a betta can have a dark outer edge on the median fins or on the tips of the pelvic fins. This usually means that the fish is still growing and is therefore a young specimen. The latter is a desirable trait only in a young fish.

The dorsal fin should also be looked at carefully. The fin should have a wide base even if it is not yet fully developed in length. The wide base will give it the potential of growing into a fin that is wide across the center with a fair amount of tissue between each fin ray. It is possible, even with a wide-based fin, that as the fish grows sufficient tissue will not develop between each fin ray. This fault, however, is usually the result of some inadequate environmental condition such as diet or temperature.

Lengthening of the pelvic fins is one of the first signs of sexual dimorphism to develop in young bettas. Sometimes these paired fins develop into thin ribbon-like structures and, as such, often tend to be carried against the fish's body. Ideally, when the fins begin to lengthen they should also begin to develop some width. White tips are quite common on the pelvic fins of bettas and do not usually cost the displayer show points. However, solid color pelvic fins, especially of a color that closely matches that of the rest of the fins, usually earn more points than the standard white-tipped pelvic fins. If a male betta has well-developed fins except for the pelvics, it is possible that some disease organisms may have attacked the pelvic fins and rotted them away. Check this fish and any other fishes in the aquarium very carefully for any signs of disease.

Relative proportions of body and fins are also important to note. A male betta having a large body and relatively short fins is probably an old fish and not a good one at that. It is doubtful that the fins of such a fish will grow much more. On the other hand, bettas having fairly well-developed but not excellent fins and a disproportionately small body may be old fish or fish that have reached sexual maturity too soon. Such fish may never catch up in their body development and will invariably lose show points. They may also be poor breeders. Bettas having a very slender body shape are not good specimens either. They may be suffering from malnutrition or may simply be the result of an inferior line. The body should be well rounded in cross-section, *slightly* rounded along the back and ever so *slightly* chunky in its overall proportions.

As your young male betta matures other characteristics will or at least should develop in certain ways. For instance, once again regarding body and fin proportions, while the fins (especially the caudal and anal fins) should be full, they should not be so full that the betta has difficulty swimming.

COLOR VARIETIES

Bettas are available in almost every color or combination of several colors imaginable, and to say that one color would be more desirable than another would be rather foolish—with such a magnificent array of colors available, selection of color in your breeders cannot be anything but a matter of pure taste. What will be done here, however, is to describe the known color types, the particular characteristics of those types that show judges look for and how the color types are inherited. This should help you make an intelligent choice of individual specimens once you have decided on a color type.

Before describing the available color strains of bettas, a description of wild bettas *(Bettas splendens)* is in order. This should help give you some understanding of how the various color strains in domesticated bettas were developed. Near the beginning of this book it was stated that domesticated bettas are so different from wild bettas in their appearance that few novice hobbyists would be able to recognize a wild betta as a betta at all. This was not an exaggeration, for wild *Betta splendens* are short-finned, relatively drab fish having a basically non-descript reddish brown body and fin color with two darker horizontal lines running the length of the body. There are some reflective blue-green markings on the body and fins and also some brighter red markings in the fins. Most of the fin markings, apart from the basic reddish brown color, seem to radiate outward from the fin bases. The pelvic fins are often more intensely red than the other fins and they usually have white tips. The intensity and   concentration of the redness and the iridescence of the blue-green color in wild bettas vary quite a bit among populations and sometimes even among individuals. Thus it can be seen that most of the colors found in today's highly domesticated bettas were present to a degree in their wild progenitors. Developing the brilliant strains seen in today's hobby was a matter of learning something of the scheme of color inheritance in these fish and developing the desired colors through selective breeding. This may sound like a simple task, but it was not. It took many years of diligent work, some of which was alluded to in the introductory pages of this book.

One of the most difficult tasks faced by the developers of pure color strains in bettas was getting pure "unpolluted" colors. To produce a blue or green betta having no obvious red pigment in the fins or body or a pure red betta having no streaks of reflective blue-green in the fins or scales was indeed a monumental task. Keeping the strains pure is not an easy job either, and this may be one reason why so many multicolored bettas are seen in hobbyists' fish rooms and in shops. There are hobbyists, of course, who like multicolored bettas. These hobbyists are not to be criticized for their preference in bettas, for there is something of a special beauty in these fish if they have good body and fin development and are of sturdy stock.

With this as our background, let us now delve into the specific known color patterns in domesticated bettas.

RED

Of all the available colors in bettas, red seems to be the most popular, or at least the most common. Red bettas have been produced in shades ranging from maroon-red to blood-red and even to a reddish orange color. Red strains have been developed in a number of different aquarium fishes, but few are equal in brilliance to red bettas. This exceptional brilliance could be an illusion created by the overall fullness of the fins. However, whether it is an illusion or not, the fact is that a red male betta appears to be one of the most spectacularly colored fish known to the hobby.

Bettas known as *normal red* are the most common kind of bettas in the hobby. These are multicolored fish having a reddish brown body and some blue or green streaks radiating into the fins from the fin bases. The basic color of the anal, dorsal, caudal and pelvic fins in these fish is red. Solid red bettas, on the other hand, are of a different genetic constitution than normal red bettas. They carry a mutation known as *extended red*. This mutation produces a fish that is entirely red except for a small area around the head. This area remains reddish brown. In a good specimen even the pectoral fins are solid red. In some specimens there may be some very slight blue or green streaking in the fins; when displayed as an extended red betta, judges tend to take points away from such a fish. The extended red form is genetically dominant to the normal red form. This means that a cross between a true-breeding extended red and a normal red will result in 100% extended red offspring. However, these offspring will not be true-breeding, and crosses between them will produce some normal reds, some non-true-breeding extended reds and some true-breeding extended reds. The problem here is that it is not possible to distinguish the true-breeding extended reds from the non-true-breeding extended reds by visual inspection. Therefore, if one wishes to maintain a line of extended reds, one must begin with male and female extended reds that are known to be true-breeding.

There is another kind of red betta known as the *red-loss*. In this strain young fish have quite a bit of red pigment, but the red breaks up and gradually disappears as the fish mature. Some red-loss bettas lose all of their red pigment while others lose only some of it.

BLUE

Like red bettas, blue bettas are also available in several different strains. The two basic types are *steel blue* and *dark blue*. The steel blue type has an overall silvery or whitish sheen, thus giving it a creamy blue color. The dominance relationship is different with steel blue bettas than it is with extended red bettas. If a betta is of the steel blue type, it can only be true-breeding. However, if it is crossed with a true-breeding normal green, all of the offspring will be of the dark blue type, thus resembling neither parent. Dark blue bettas, however, cannot breed true. Thus if a dark blue is mated to a dark blue, some of the offspring will be steel blue, some will be dark blue and some will be normal green. As far as color is concerned, a dark blue betta can be a bright iridescent blue or a dark blue color depending upon how much iridescence the fish carries in its genes; the less iridescence, the darker the blue. Some dark blue strains tend to be almost purple in color.

GREEN

There are also two types of green bettas, the *normal greens* and the *metallic greens*. In normal green bettas there may be quite a bit of red, reddish brown or blue showing through the iridescent green pigment. The green in this strain is limited to spots on the scales and rays of green projecting from the fin bases into the fins. In metallic green bettas the metallic green iridescence is spread all over the fins and body except in the area of the head. As in most bettas, the head area tends to remain reddish brown, although there have been some exceptions with this and other color strains. In these exceptional bettas the body color covers the head as well.

A mating between a pair of normal green bettas produces all normal green offspring, and all bettas of the normal green type are true-breeding. When true-breeding metallic greens are bred to one another, they also produce all true-breeding replicas of themselves. However, when a metallic green is crossed to a normal green, all of the offspring are non-true-breeding metallic greens. When non-true-breeding metallic greens (which, like the non-true-breeding ex-

54

tended reds; cannot be visually distinguished from their true-breeding counterparts) are bred to one another some of their offspring will be true-breeding metallic greens, some will be non-true-breeding metallic greens and some will be normal greens. No matter which way metallic green bettas are arrived at, however, they all have a nearly solid sparkling green or aquamarine color.

YELLOW

Yellow in bettas can range from a creamy whitish yellow or straw yellow to an orangish or brownish yellow, the latter sometimes being known as the honey betta. There are two kinds of yellow bettas, too. One is called the *normal yellow* betta and usually results from the loss of other pigments such as blue, green or black, thus exposing the underlying yellow pigment. These are usually multicolored bettas. Most solid yellow bettas, however, result from a genetic mutation in which yellow pigment is substituted for red pigment. These are known as *non-red* bettas. They breed true, but when they are crossed with bettas of other colors, especially reds, the other colors usually predominate. In other words, they are genetically recessive to red and perhaps to other colors as well.

BLACK

Finally, concerning solid-colored bettas, there are the blacks. Solid black in bettas is one of the least understood color phenomena in these fish. As in most of the other solid-colored bettas there are also two types of blacks. One is the *normal black*, which is actually another type of multicolored betta. In these fish the black pigment is not very dense and the fish more often than not show a lot of dark blue or dark green coloration. Normal black is the genetically dominant black type, while the other type, the *melano*, is recessive to normal black. This means that a pure normal black bred to a pure normal black will produce nothing but pure normal black offspring. However, a different situation arises with the melano, which is a much blacker fish then the normal black. Melano offspring cannot be produced from a mating between a pair of melanos because female melanos have so far proved to be infertile. Melano males can be bred to normal black females, and this mating will produce some normal black males and females and some melano males and females. Remember, however, that the melano females so produced are infertile. To put it more specifically, melano females do produce eggs, but the eggs seem to be incapable of being fertilized. As long as there are normal black female bettas carrying the recessive gene or genes for the melano trait and there are both normal black and melano black males, we will continue to see densely colored melano black bettas. Care must be taken that we do not lose the melano strain, for if we do, then we must wait for another random mutation for melano to occur—and that may be a very long time! For more information on this unique strain of bettas see "The Mystery of the Black Betta" by Dr. Sue Liebetrau, an article that appeared in the February, 1979 issue of *Tropical Fish Hobbyist* magazine.

CAMBODIAN

There are other multicolored betta strains besides those mentioned thus far. One of the most popular is the *Cambodian*. In this strain the fish usually totally lack black pigment except in the eyes. The body of a Cambodian betta is a creamy whitish or pinkish color and the fins are red, blue or green, although red is by far the most common type. The finnage in most Cambodians is solid colored, but occasionally some show up that have multicolored fins as in the normal reds or the normal greens. One of the primary qualities looked for in Cambodian bettas by show judges is an unmarked body. Less favored Cambodians may have some black, red or iridescent pigment on the body, especially near the fin bases. This "color pollution" can be eliminated by proper selective breeding, but it will return quickly if the strain is not carefully maintained.

Cambodian bettas breed true; that is, when they are bred to one another they produce only Cambodian offspring. However, if a Cambodian is crossed with nearly any other color strain, the trait will be obscured in all the offspring. A small percentage of Cambodians will arise again in the following generation if the first generation offspring are bred to one another; these Cambodians will remain true-breeding.

MARBLE

One of the least understood strains, genetically speaking, is the marble or piebald betta. These fish are covered with patches of black pigment in varying densities. The specific pattern is usually not consistently repetitive and it changes almost constantly as the fish grows. Changes in the pattern may even be observed from day to day. The black patches may be seen on the body and on the fins and may be found in areas of blue, green, red or yellow pigment. The black patches may also be found on fins that otherwise totally lack any pigment.

BUTTERFLY

A good quality butterfly betta is one of the most magnificent of all of the multicolor strains. Like the marble betta, the butterfly betta has patches of pigment, but in this strain the patches are red, not black, and are generally confined to the fins only. The body of the butterfly betta is like that of a Cambodian, a creamy whitish or pinkish color. In good show specimens the body color (or lack of color) extends into the median fin bases. The red patches extend from a short distance beyond the fin base to a short distance from the outer edges of the fins. The remaining tissue from the patches of red to the outer edges of the fins is the same color as the area between the body and the patches. In other words, the fins contain large patches of red that are surrounded by translucent or whitish tissue. Specimens that lose show points are those in which the red patches extend all the way to the dorsal and ventral edges of the caudal fin and inward through the fin bases to the body. Specimens showing any red markings on the body generally also lose points. Genetically speaking, the butterfly trait is dominant over the normal red trait, but this is not a case of simple dominance. It is complicated by other gene actions that cause the amount of red on the fins to vary from very small patches to complete fin coverage. Butterflies having the latter pattern are almost indistinguishable from normal red Cambodian bettas.

FIN VARIETIES

Long-fin

All of the bettas discussed so far, except the wild ones, have been of the *long-finned* variety. Any time a *short-finned* wild betta is bred to a long-finned betta, the offspring will all resemble the long-finned parent in fin shape. This is because the long-finned trait is the result of a genetic mutation that is dominant over the short-finned trait. If brothers and sisters of this cross are bred together, some of their offspring will have the long-finned trait and some will have the short-finned trait. Of these long-finned offspring, however, only a portion of them will be true-breeding long-finned fish, but those that are not true-breeding will not be distinguishable from those that are.

Among long-finned bettas there is quite a bit of variance in the length of the fins. Some of that variance is naturally due to heredity, but as discussed earlier, much of it is the result of environmental differences such as diet, temperature, water chemistry, age at which the fish are isolated and age at which they are allowed to breed. Providing bettas with the correct environmental conditions as described earlier in this book reduces the amount of variance in fin length due to the environment, thus most of the variance seen in fin length will be due to hereditary factors. This aids the breeder in improving his bettas by genetic selection. Of course, it is understood that when speaking of long fins versus short fins we are speaking of fin length in males only. Females carrying the long-finned trait have short fins very similar to those of wild male and female bettas.

Double-Tail

The *double-tail* trait is one of the most interesting fin mutations to arise in domesticated bettas, for it is a complex mutation affecting not only the shape of the caudal fin, but also that of the dorsal fin and the body. The novice, upon first seeing a double-tail betta, can easily mistake it for a betta that has been injured, having the tail split down the middle all the way to the fin base. However, it is not an injury. It is a mutation in which the caudal fin is divided into two lobes, an upper lobe and a lower lobe. Unlike the forked tail of a characoid or a catfish in which the caudal fin is merely notched from the posterior edge toward the caudal peduncle, the caudal fin of the double-tail betta is divided all the way to the caudal peduncle. The depth of this division does vary somewhat, but even on those bettas whose tails are not divided all the way down to the peduncle, the bifurcation is much deeper than it is on any fish having merely a forked tail.

Because of the nature of the division in the tail, the double-tail betta seems to have a stubbier body than its single-tailed counterpart. In some fish this may be only an illusion due to the split in the tail, but in others the caudal peduncle is distinctly thickened dorso-ventrally. This thickening definitely gives the fish an overall stubby appearance, even in specimens having exceptionally long fins.

The dorsal fin is also affected by the double-tail mutation. The number of dorsal fin rays is greatly increased, giving the fin a much longer base. The insertion of the fin into the body, therefore, lies much further forward in the double-tail betta than it does in the single-tail betta. The first ray in the dorsal fin of the double-tail betta lies almost opposite the first ray of the anal fin, whereas in the normal single-tailed betta the first ray of the dorsal fin lies approximately opposite the center fin rays of the anal fin. In addition to the great increase in the number of dorsal fin rays in this fish, there is also a vast increase in the length of these rays, thus giving the fish a much longer and fuller dorsal fin than that of the normal betta. The increased length varies among individuals and among breeding lines, but in some specimens the fin is so long that it actually drapes far over the tail. This draping effect reminds one of the hi-fin trait in some swordtails and platies, but it may be even more exaggerated in some bettas.

The double-tail trait has been bred into almost every known color strain of bettas. The one that appears in the hobby most frequently, however, seems to be the honey double-tail. This fish is a tannish yellow or honey color.

The double-tail trait is not characteristic of males only, but it is quite evident in females too. While the actual dorsal fin length in the double-tail female is not necessarily increased as it is in the male, the length of the fin base is greatly increased, just as in the male. As a matter of fact, the dorsal fin of a double-tail female betta looks more like that of a gourami of the genus *Colisa* or of a cichlid than it does like a normal betta.

The double-tail mutation is recessive to normal fins whether they are long or short. Therefore in a cross between a long-finned betta and a double-tail betta all of the offspring will have long fins and no doubled tail. In the next generation the double-tail mutation will again arise but only in some of the offspring. Double-tails bred to double-tails will produce nothing but double-tail offspring, for fish showing the mutation are true-breeding.

It has been the experience of some hobbyists that double-tail bettas are just a bit more delicate than their single-tail counterparts. With just a little bit of extra effort hobbyists have, however, been quite successful in maintaining this strain.

Combtail

In this trait the rays of the fins are longer than the tissue between the rays. In a good specimen this ray elongation is uniform throughout all the median fins. When properly proportioned, the trait gives the fish a comb-like look to the fins, especially the tail. The length of the elongated rays can vary from individual to individual and from breeding line to breeding line. In a poor specimen the ray elongation is not regular and the fish has a very ragged appearance. Ragged combtail bettas do not take very many points in a show.

Like the double-tail trait, the combtail trait shows in females and males and has been bred into many color strains in the hobby. Very little is known of the genetics of this trait.

While some of the basic mechanics of inheritance in bettas were discussed in this chapter, detailed explanations of betta genetics were intentionally avoided. If one has some understanding of the basics of simple Mendelian genetics, what is so far known of inheritance in bettas is not hard to understand, but without that basic background the subject can be a bit difficult to grasp. Since the purpose of this book is to provide the reader with the basics of keeping and breeding bettas rather than to provide information on developing new strains, and because of the limited space herein, I therefore have chosen not to provide the fine details of betta genetics. The small amount of general genetic information provided here, however, should be sufficient to allow most hobbyists to maintain the integrity of the strains they have chosen to keep and perhaps even to improve them a bit.

A male betta gathers fertilized eggs and places them in his bubblenest. **Below:** A male betta's display usually attracts a female that is ready to spawn. Photos by R. Zukal.

Breeding Bettas

Bettas, like a great many other anabantoids, build a floating nest of bubbles in which the eggs and larvae are incubated. The nest, usually built by the male alone, is composed of mucus-coated bubbles and bits of floating plant debris. The eggs and the fry are dutifully tended to by the male, who keeps them in the bubblenest.

It is not difficult to induce bettas to spawn, but the hard part is raising the fry. The fry are very small and are consequently difficult to feed. In addition, they are quite delicate and require very special precautions on the part of the hobbyist in order to bring them through their first few weeks of life. However, once the aquarist understands the require-

ments of bettas, they are not difficult to breed and it is not that difficult to raise the fry.

THE AQUARIUM

An aquarium as small as five gallons will do, although a 10-gallon tank is more ideal, as it gives the female more room to escape from the male during his rather aggressive courtship. The tank should be thoroughly sterilized using a strong salt solution. It is important that the tank have a tight-fitting cover in order to eliminate cool drafts over the water and to help retain a warm moist atmosphere between the aquarium top and the water surface. The reasons for this precaution will be dealt with later.

PLANTS

Betta courtship is extremely aggressive on the part of the male, and in selecting plants for the breeding tank one should consider the shelter they will provide for the female. A few thick bunches of cabomba *(Cabomba caroliniana)* or hornwort *(Ceratophyllum)* should be placed in the rear corners of the tank and perhaps along the back. The female will be able to seek refuge among the bushy fronds, and the fine leaves of these plants will provide plenty of support material for the male to use in the construction of the bubblenest. The plants can be anchored in place by planting them in gravel contained in small clay flowerpots.

GRAVEL

With the exception of the flowerpots mentioned above, it is best to keep the bottom of the betta breeding tank bare. A layer of gravel makes it more difficult for the male to find the fertilized eggs which sink to the bottom during the spawning embrace. In addition, the gravel can harbor microorganisms and uneaten food particles that could cause a problem for the developing eggs. Because the tank must be kept very clean, the absence of gravel makes cleaning the bottom easy and causes fewer disturbances to the brooding male.

THE WATER

The condition of the water can be the difference between failure and success in breeding bettas. The pH ideally should be slightly acidic to neutral (6.8 to 7.0). The water should be fairly soft (8 to 10 degrees of hardness or DH). This condition can be achieved in two ways. A 50%-50% mixture of distilled or demineralized water and tapwater usually produces water of the required hardness. Another way to achieve the correct chemistry is to condition the water before putting the breeders into the tank. This can be done by filtering it through peat moss until the desired levels of pH and DH are reached. The procedure for this was discussed earlier in the chapter on aquarium conditions.

FILTRATION

An inside box filter or a sponge filter is the best kind to use in a betta breeding tank. Either of these will adequately aerate the water while keeping it clean. Polyester floss is the best material to use in the filter. The filter should be run very gently so as not to create much of a disturbance at the surface of the water, otherwise the bubblenest will be disturbed and possibly broken up. In addition, too much circulation makes it more difficult for the male to keep the eggs and fry in the nest. Some hobbyists prefer to alternately run the filter for a few hours and then shut it off for a few hours. It should be shut off at least during feeding so that food particles do not become trapped in the filter where their decomposition could pollute the water, creating problems for the eggs and fry. If all uneaten food is siphoned out of the tank a few minutes after feeding the fish, then there is no need to worry about food particles becoming trapped in the filter. As an extra precaution, however, if a box filter

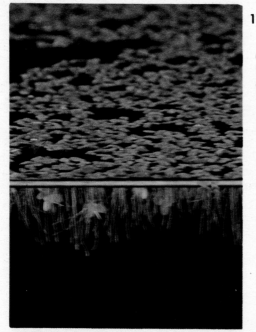

(1) *Lemna,* commonly known as duckweed, is an excellent plant for bubblenest builders, as its short fine roots help strengthen the nest. (2) A nest of bubbles can be seen in the middle of this cluster of *Salvinia* leaves. Photo by Dr. Herbert R. Axelrod. (3) *Cabomba* is another useful plant for spawning bettas. Floating fronds or floating broken leaves make good nesting material and planted clusters provide good cover for females. Photos 1 and 3 by R. Zukal.

is being used the top can be left off once all of the air bubbles are out of the filter floss. Then the fish can swim into the filter to eat any food particles that settle there. This technique is especially useful in the fry-rearing tank.

TEMPERATURE CONTROL

It is imperative that constant heat be maintained in the breeding tank, for the fry, as mentioned earlier, are exceptionally delicate for the first few weeks. Fluctuating temperatures can cause their demise. A good quality, properly installed, thermostatically controlled aquarium heater should be used.

Most hobbyists prefer to keep the water level rather low in the breeding tank. This makes it easier for struggling new fry to get back to the surface where they must remain for a while until the labyrinth organ develops. If you are not using a specially built shallow tank to accommodate this need, then the water level should be dropped in the standard tank. If this is the case, make sure that the water level is not more than an inch or two below the top of the heater tube, otherwise temperature control will be erratic. This is one reason for having a tight-fitting top—it helps maintain steadier heat when the water level is dropped.

If you wish to maintain a lower water level than is practical for correct heater operation, there is a rather simple method to bring about good heat control. Use a submersible heater, one that is specifically engineered to be submerged. There are several brands available.

Temperatures between 80 and 85°F. are suitable for breeding bettas, but a temperature of about 82°F. usually produces the best results. Although the fish breed well at 85°F., the eggs develop too rapidly at that temperature; this has been known to cause weak fry.

CONDITIONING THE BREEDERS

Bettas are not necessarily seasonal spawners. If they are

68

ripe, they can be spawned almost any time conditions are right. In order for a female to develop enough ripe eggs to enable her to spawn, she must be given an abundance of highly nutritious foods. A concentration of high quality foods also helps condition the male for breeding. Conditioning can be carried out in the breeding tank while keeping the breeders separated by a glass or plastic partition. Frequent small feedings using as much live food as possible will quickly bring the breeders into spawning condition. Because so much food is being introduced during this time and because so much waste is being produced by the fish, extra cleaning efforts are necessary during the conditioning period.

NESTBUILDING

Although the male may begin to build a bubblenest without a female being within his sight, the presence of a female, especially a well-rounded ripe one, on the other side of a transparent partition usually stimulates the male into intense nestbuilding activity. Some hobbyists use a transparent plastic partition that is drilled full of small holes, for it is believed that the sense of smell as well as the sense of sight plays a role in stimulating the male into building a nest. If one wishes to ignore the olfactory sense for lack of a suitable partition (many hobbyists are successful without it), the female can be placed in a jar of water which is then placed in the breeding tank. An aerator or sponge filter should be used in the jar.

One of the problems created by the partition when spawning time finally arrives is that its removal from the tank in order to bring the spawners together can break up the nest if the male builds it against the partition. Providing some fine-leaved plants on the male's side of the tank and anchoring them in such a way that they either float on the surface or grow up to the surface at the tank wall opposite the partition often stimulates the male into building his

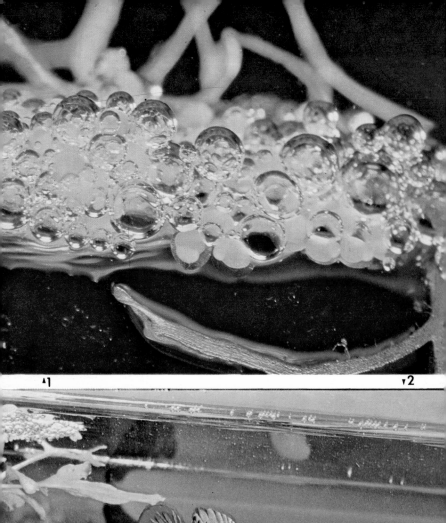

(1) A bubblenest constructed among the leaves of a clump of *Riccia fluitans*. (2) Courtship and mating occurs in *Betta imbellis* in about the same way as it does in the more familiar *Betta slendens*. (3) A pair of *Betta imbellis* spawn under a bubblenest. (4) A ripe female *Betta splendens* hovers under the bubblenest as she awaits the male's return for spawning. Photos by H.J. Richter.

nest there. In that case removal of the partition will not break up the nest. Otherwise, the partition or jar cannot be removed. If that is the case, then the female must be netted and placed in the male's portion of the tank.

As the female's abdomen begins to swell, the male's courting activity becomes very intense. When the female swims near the partition the male approaches from his side, spreads his fins, flares out his opercula or gill covers, extends the dark red branchiostegal membranes from under the gill covers and twists his body into an "S" shape. During this display his color intensifies tremendously and his fins spread so widely that sometimes it seems as if they are going to split apart. If the female is nearly ready to spawn, she often responds to the male's actions by returning a similar display. The male then returns to the nest and continues his nest-building activity more vigorously than ever.

The male betta's nest-building activity is a fascinating phenomenon to watch. The male swims to the surface, takes a gulp of air and spits out a mucus-coated air bubble. He then quickly takes another bubble of air and releases it near the first one. This process continues for hours with occasional breaks to search for food or to court the female. After a while the nest begins to take on a definite shape. The male may hold a single position for about 15 to 20 minutes, swinging only his head and the front part of his body from side to side as he takes a bubble of air, swings under the nest to release the bubble and swings back to the edge of the nest to take in another bubble of air. A highly stimulated male may complete his nest in a few hours, but often he may take a few days to finish it. Actually, the nest never is completely finished, for the male intermittently adds bubbles to it during the courting period, sometimes between spawning embraces and during the egg and fry incubation period.

The nest often has an almost discoidal shape, being three to four inches in diameter and rising as much as half an inch out of the water. However, the shape and size of the nest varies. Some males may build a nest that has no particular shape and covers almost the entire surface of a small aquarium, while others may build a nest no larger than an inch or two in diameter. Once the breeding pair is placed together the active courtship and spawning activity may cause parts of the nest to break up. The male usually stops what he is doing and repairs the nest. The shape of the nest may change from day to day or even hour to hour as repairs and rebuilding continue.

SPAWNING BEHAVIOR

When the nest is fairly complete and the male begins to spend more time courting the female than he does working on the nest, it is time to place the pair together, provided the female's abdomen is well rounded. Now an extremely intense and often rough courtship begins. The male very aggressively pursues the female, attempting to entice her under the nest. In his efforts to bring her to the nest he can be quite brutal if she doesn't willingly respond. More often than not, by the time the first spawning embrace begins the female's fins are quite badly torn and she may even be missing some scales.

When the female is finally ready to spawn she aproaches the male under the nest, swimming toward him in an oblique, head-down position with her fins closed against her body. She more or less gyrates her body as she swims toward him. This approach seems to signal the male that she is ready to spawn and he approaches her more gently than he does during earlier parts of the courtship. Before the first spawning embrace begins, there may be a few more mutual displays under the nest, during which time the colors of both fish become very intense, with the female showing an obscure barred body pattern. With fins spread and colors flashing the pair gyrate in a side by side position. The fish circle one another, nudging each other in the sides

1

A spawning sequence in *Betta splendens.* (1) The male encircles the female under the bubblenest. (2) Eggs and sperm are expelled simultaneously. (3) The male begins to gather eggs as the nuptial embrace terminates. (4) Following the embrace, the female floats in an almost catatonic state for a few seconds as the male busily gathers eggs which he will carefully place in the bubblenest. Photos by H.J. Richter.

2

with their snouts. Finally the female begins to turn upside down and the male wraps himself around the female more or less in a "U" shape. With their vents in close apposition, as many as 50 eggs are expelled and fertilized. The eggs slowly sink as the pair gently disengages from the embrace. Then the female floats toward the top, seemingly paralyzed. The male begins to gather the whitish eggs in his mouth as the female recovers from the embrace. Sometimes the female helps the male gather the eggs. Taking a few eggs at a time to the nest, the fish blow them up into the mass of bubbles. However, usually the female retreats altogether and must be reenticed to the nest by the male. When the entire spawning activity appears to have terminated it is best to remove the female from the tank, for the male will now try to keep her away from the nest and in doing so may become quite violent. The female should be placed in a quiet, clean quarantine tank in order to recover from the injuries she has sustained during spawning. Her recovery can be assisted by the addition of a mild dose of methylene blue or non-iodized salt to the water. Methylene blue is available as a commercially prepared fish medication. If salt is used, about one teaspoon to a gallon of water is sufficient.

BROODING BEHAVIOR

The brooding behavior of the male betta is quite remarkable. He spends most of his time under the nest, patching it and pushing the developing eggs back into it as they occasionally fall out. Sometimes he moves the eggs to firmer parts of the nest. Once spawning is over and all of the eggs are in the nest, it is not unusual for the male to build an entirely new nest in another part of the tank and move all of the eggs into it.

The eggs hatch in 24 to 48 hours, depending upon the temperature of the water. The young hang tail-down in the nest for about 36 hours while they absorb the remainder of the yolk material. Many of them fall from the nest during this period, but the male is always there to pick them up and place them back into the nest. When the yolk sac is entirely absorbed the young begin to swim in a horizontal position and start to wander from the nest. The male constantly attempts to herd the young back to the nest area and it is at this time that the male should be removed from the tank, for he may soon begin to eat the fry.

None of the behavior patterns discussed in this chapter should be interpreted as being absolutely rigid and unvarying. As mentioned above, there may be differences in the length of time it takes the male to build the nest and in the size and shape of the nest. Sometimes a male may use no supporting material in the nest at all, and at other times he may use an abundance of plant material. Occasionally a female may be more aggressive during courtship, and sometimes, even though well rounded in the belly, she may not respond to the male at all. There have been occasions documented when the courtship was a gentle affair with both partners willingly participating in all phases of courtship, spawning and brooding. On the other hand, there have been some occasions when, after the bubblenest was constructed, neither partner was willing to spawn. There may be times when the male offers no brood care at all; instead, he eats the eggs. By and large, however, the courtship, spawning and brooding behavior described here is usually followed rather closely.

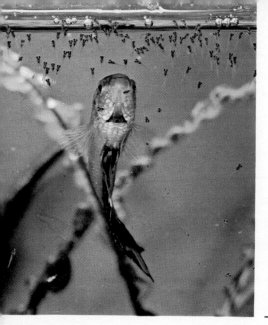

A male betta tends to a brood of fry that are just beginning to swim free. This is the time that the male should be removed from the breeding tank. **Below:** Betta fry hang head-up in the bubblenest until their yolk sacs are completely absorbed. Photos by H.J. Richter.

Raising the Fry

The few weeks that follow the male's removal from the breeding tank is the most critical time for the fry. To begin with, they are quite small and require an abundance of very small foods. Some hobbyists use an egg-yolk infusion to feed the fry at this stage. This is done by straining the yolk of a hard-boiled egg through a clean linen handkerchief. The fine particles squeezed through the cloth are about the right size for betta fry. This is, however, a messy process that can easily lead to a foul tank and dead fry if extra care is not taken to siphon out all uneaten food, and that is not easy to do without also siphoning out the fry.

An alternative to feeding egg-yolk to new betta fry is to

feed them from an infusoria culture. This is a culture of microorganisms consisting of *Paramecium, Euglena* and many other kinds of organisms that are too small to be seen by the naked eye. These organisms can be seen and eaten by all betta fry. If the breeding aquarium is set up properly, many of these organisms will already be living in the aquarium by the time the young bettas are ready to begin feeding. However, they can be raised in a culture by infusing with hay or soft lettuce leaves a jar of old aquarium water siphoned from the bottom of a well-established aquarium. It takes a few days for the culture to develop, so it should be started when the betta conditioning begins. A few eyedroppers of water from the infusoria culture will be enough for one feeding of the fry, and they should be fed as often as possible. Feeding the fry six to eight times a day is not too much. To be assured of having enough food in each dropperful it is helpful to shine a light on one spot in the culture jar for a few minutes before removing the culture water for feeding. The water should be removed from the area into which the light was shining. The same idea can be employed in the tank containing the fry, for the light will attract both the infusorians and the fry. After a few days of feeding on infusorians the fry can be switched over to newly hatched brine shrimp and finely ground dry foods.

There are some hobbyists who feed young bettas newly hatched brine shrimp as their first food rather than using infusorians or an egg-yolk infusion. They have found that new baby bettas are capable of tearing newly hatched brine shrimp apart. Admittedly some of the baby bettas will not be able to handle this as their first food and will perish if nothing else is offered, but hobbyists who use this method feel that they would rather raise 10 or 20 strong competitive bettas than an abundance of moderate-size weaker specimens. It basically boils down to a matter of personal choice. Much more detailed information on culturing infusorians and hatching brine shrimp is available in the book

Encyclopedia of Live Foods mentioned earlier in this book.

During the critical period when the fry are feeding heavily on small organisms, they are also developing the labyrinth organ in the head. During this time the fry are extremely sensitive to cool drafts passing over the water surface of the aquarium. Therefore, a tight-fitting aquarium cover is essential to success in raising young bettas. The cover keeps warm moist air over the water, which allows the babies to take gulps of air without damaging the developing labyrinth organ. A damaged labyrinth will cause the fry to die. After the fry are two or three weeks old the cover can be gradually withdrawn, exposing about an inch more of space to the atmosphere every few days.

It is best not to move fry during this critical period. The fish should therefore be bred in a tank large enough to support a few hundred fry until they are about a month old. At that time it is usually safe to move them. If the fry must be moved at an earlier age, it is best to drop the water level to an inch or two in the breeding tank and gently pour the fry into the larger tank rather than netting them out. Netting them out of the water also can damage the developing labyrinth organ.

Most hobbyists who breed any fishes breed them for the challenge of having a successful spawning and to acquire a few more specimens of the species. Unless the hobbyist is an experienced breeder with lots of tank space and the intention to raise bettas on a commercial or semi-commercial basis, it is best to cull the young, keeping only enough to fill the available tank space without crowding them. It is much more rewarding to raise a few fine specimens than it is to raise hundreds of inferior specimens. Culling can begin when the fish are about a month old, before their first move. In selecting one-month-old bettas for a larger rearing tank, one can only select them on the basis of size and deportment, for they don't begin to show very much of their color and ultimate fin shape until they are about three

1 (1) A black double-tail male betta. (2) A yellow double-tail male betta.
(3) This prize-winning black lace male was bred by Sue Liebetrau.
The smoky fin color is typical of the black lace strain. Photos by Al
Liebetrau.

▲2   ▼3

(1) A close-up of a male betta placing a straggling baby back into the bubblenest. Photo by W.R. Kraft. (2) After a few weeks of good feeding, baby bettas begin to take on the typical betta shape. (3) This is the joyful result of putting in a lot of extra effort to raise fine bettas. Trophies like this are awarded all over the country for top betta specimens.

months old. During the first move all of the runts and deformed specimens should be discarded. A 25 or 30-gallon aquarium is adequate for raising about 50 to 75 one-month-old fry to the age of about three months, at which time they can be partially culled for size and color. At about this time males begin to fight with one another, so it is necessary to separate each one into its own container. One-gallon jars or, better yet, 2½-gallon aquariums should be used to house each male. Females can be kept together in the large rearing tank, as they do not fight with one another nearly as much as do males. At three months of age sexing bettas is quite easy; the males are usually more brightly colored and they have longer fins than the females.

The photo to the left shows a female extended red double-tail betta. This fish was bred by Mr. and Mrs. L. Bickel and photographed by Al Liebetrau. **Below:** A fine example of an extended red double-tail male betta. Photo courtesy of Wardley Products Co.

The Betta Room

Hobbyists whose enthusiasm for bettas causes them to become betta specialists soon find themselves inundated with bowls, jars and tanks of bettas everywhere. At this point, if one is to continue his or her pursuit and perhaps even produce some stock for sale in local shops, it will be necessary to set up a "bettary."

A room devoted to the propagation of bettas need not be large, elaborate or expensive in order to be functional. The most important consideration is having enough heat and a good heat control system. It was mentioned earlier in this book that in order to keep bettas in prime condition they must be kept at about 80° F. This is not difficult with an ordinary aquarium heater, but when you have as many small

containers as you will have in your betta room, keeping them warm is not so easy. It would certainly not be very practical to raise the temperature in your home to 80° F to accommodate your bettas. However, since a room as small as six feet by four feet could be adequate for raising hundreds of bettas in individual jars, it would not take a very expensive space heater to keep the temperature in that small room up to an adequate level and well controlled, too. It is most important for good heat control that the room be well insulated with at least four inches of insulation hung on the walls. Inexpensive 1/8-inch masonite sheets are more than adequate for lining the inside of the room and holding the insulation in place between the studs. The 80° F temperature maintained in this room will be fine for maintaining small unheated rearing containers. In order to raise the heat in the breeding tanks a little higher than the room temperature, standard aquarium heaters can be employed. Using a system such as this, you need not have banks of electric aquarium heaters to keep your bettas warm.

There is another way to keep small betta-rearing containers warm enough without having individual heaters for each one of them. Partially fill a large shallow aquarium with water and place the filled betta jars down into the water. The tank can then be filled to within an inch of the tops of the betta jars. Now simply place an aquarium heater in this tank and make sure that the water is thoroughly circulated around the outside of the jars by providing a strong stream of bubbles from several airstones. Raise the temperature of the water outside the jars to the desired level and this will maintain the water in the jars at about the same temperature. In this way only one aquarium heater is used to maintain the heat in six to twelve jars depending upon the size of the tank and the size of the jars. It is best to use a submersible heater for this setup. In most aquaria the water level would have to be maintained too low for the proper operation of heaters that hang over the side of the tank.

There is, however, a way to get around this problem too. Place bricks between the jars and the bottom of the aquarium. This will elevate the jars sufficiently to allow the aquarium to be filled high enough for proper heater operation.

One of the advantages of using drum bowls or half or one-gallon jars for rearing individual bettas is that a bank of these containers distributes the weight of the water over a wider area than it would be spread if the fish were kept in larger aquaria. This means that less expensive materials can be used as shelving to hold the betta containers. I have found that lightweight steel shelf sets, the kind that are sold in discount department stores, are the most practical for use as shelving units in betta rooms. The shelves can be adjusted to any desired height easily and quickly, and a four-foot-long shelf holds up to a dozen jars, depending upon which size jar you use. These units are strong and durable, and compared to custom-made wood shelving of the same size, they are much cheaper. Furthermore, if you ever decide to get out of the betta hobby, you'll find many other uses for the steel shelving units.

As far as containers are concerned, one-gallon flat-sided drum bowls are fine for rearing individual male bettas to maturity. They have an advantage over cylindrical jars in that the bettas can be viewed without the distortion produced by the round sides of the jars, if the flat sides are placed to the front and rear of the shelf. If space is a consideration, however, the bowls may have to be placed with flat sides adjacent to one another and the curved sides facing outward. Viewing bettas through these curved sides makes them appear much more distorted than they would appear through the sides of cylindrical jars. This would not be a problem if the shelves were wide enough to allow two rows of drum bowls to be placed in front of each other in a staggered manner so that all the bettas could be seen without moving the bowls around.

▲1 ▼2

3 (1) The red patch in the dorsal fin of this butterfly betta shows a clean break from the fin base, but the red patches in the caudal and anal fin do not break away as cleanly. The ideal butterfly betta would show the clean break in all the median fins. Photo by S. Frank. (2) Dr. Gene Lucas developed this white opaque strain. This betta was owned by Mr. and Mrs. Ted Williams and photographed by Al Liebetrau. (3) This is a honey double-tail betta. Photo courtesy of Wardley Products Co.

If space is a big factor, cleaned one-gallon pickle jars are the next best thing. Smaller jars can indeed be used, but the water in them must be changed more often than is practical, especially if several hundred jars are being maintained. This brings up the question of where you get hundreds of pickle jars: either eat a lot of pickles or make an arrangement with a restaurant to save their pickle and mayonnaise jars. Many restaurant owners are happy to give the jars away, while others see this as an opportunity to make a little bit of extra profit. Even if you have to buy the jars, a restaurant will rarely charge more than $.25 or $.50 a piece for them.

Cleaning the jars for use as aquaria is not difficult. First they should be washed out with soap and warm water as thoroughly as possible. The jar labels usually come loose as the jars are washed. If they do not, they can be scraped off with a single-edged razor blade. After thoroughly rinsing the jars, fill them with warm water and dissolve three or four heaping tablespoons of baking soda in them. The jars should be soaked for at least a few hours—overnight is even better. Before using the jars, make sure that all of the soap and baking soda are rinsed out of them. It doesn't take very much residual soap scum to poison a betta. The baking soda treatment will rid the jars of all residual pickle juice or mayonnaise. After one treatment all odors should be gone, but if there is the slightest odor of pickles or mayonnaise in the jars, repeat the treatment. Be very careful that all of the food particles and juices are removed from the threaded area of the jars where the tops screw on. *All jar lids should be discarded!* They are usually made of metal which can corrode and poison your fish, but even if they are plastic, they are impossible to get clean enough.

Because of the betta's labyrinth organ, these fish can be maintained in small jars without providing them with extra aeration from an airstone and pump if the jars are kept immaculately clean. This means that every bit of uneaten food must be removed as soon as the fish have finished eating. This also means daily cleaning of accumulations of feces and weekly water changes which entail changing at least half of the water in each jar at one time, and more if possible. This necessitates the use of aged water that has been dechlorinated using one of the anti-chlorine compounds sold in pet shops. Aged water in this case is a bit better since it will have had a chance to stabilize chemically in the storage vessel.

If all of these conditions are met, betta jars need not be filtered. However, if you prefer to use filters, small sponge filters work best in small containers. The sponge filter works as both a particulate separator and a biological filter, with the porosity of the sponge providing a vast amount of surface area on which the beneficial bacteria colonies can become established. These filters should be cleaned by siphoning the dirt accumulations off their outside surfaces, but the filters should not be washed, because washing will destroy the established bacteria colonies. These filters can be used almost indefinitely without removing them from the jars to wash them if proper maintenance procedures are followed in keeping the jars clean. Remember what was said earlier about bettas and water currents. Don't run the sponge filters very strongly or your bettas will do little else but lie around the bottom of the bowls or jars.

No book on bettas can be complete without at least mentioning the International Betta Congress. This is an international organization consisting of hundreds of hobbyists who are betta specialists. There are many advantages to belonging to such an organization. One is the sanctioning of betta shows at which you may display the fruits of your labors and have the opportunity to be rewarded for your efforts by winning trophies in competition against other betta breeders. The organization and its shows offer the opportunity to meet and correspond with other betta enthusiasts and to learn the secrets of their successes and failures.